THE

BEATITUDES
(A Study Guide for Children)

CATHERINE A GARRETT

CONTENTS

3

ACKNOWLEDGEMENTS

This book would not be possible without the encouragement and support of my family and friends.

I would also like to thank my talented friend Amanda, who worked diligently on the wonderful artwork for this book.

Finally and foremost, I thank my Lord and Savior Jesus Christ. I am truly blessed to have had the opportunity to write this study guide and look forward to see how God will use it for His Glory.

THE BEATITUDES

MATTHEW 5:1-11

"Now when He saw the crowds, He went up on a mountainside and sat down. His disciples came to Him, and he began to teach them, saying:

BLESSED are the poor in spirit,
     For theirs is the kingdom of heaven.

BLESSED are those who mourn,
     For they shall be comforted.

BLESSED are the meek,
     For they shall inherit the earth.

BLESSED are those who hunger and thirst for righteousness,
     For they will be filled.

BLESSED are the merciful,
     For they will be shown mercy.

BLESSED are the pure in heart,
     For they shall see God.

BLESSED are the peacemakers,
     For they shall be called sons of God.

BLESSED are those who are persecuted because of righteousness,

    For theirs is the kingdom of heaven.

BLESSED are you when people insult you, persecute you and falsely say all kinds of evil against you because of me, rejoice and be glad, because great is your reward in heaven,

    For in the same way they persecuted the prophets who were before you."

INTRODUCTION

Humans are a lot like toy boxes. Both are filled with brokenness. I bet if you look at the bottom of your toy boxes, you would find bits and pieces of broken toys that several Christmas' ago, you thought were the best gifts you've ever received. It's possible that some of these broken toys could be repaired or fixed to be used again, but others may be unfixable and have to be thrown away. From your favorite army tank, baby doll or video equipment, nothing in this world is perfect. Eventually it will wear out or break and have to be tossed out with the trash. Humans are not perfect either.

Beginning with Adam and Eve when they disobeyed God by eating from the tree of good and evil, the human race has been morally and spiritually broken.

ROMANS 15:21

"For as in Adam all die, so in Christ all will be made alive."

You were born with a sin nature and as a result, you have been separated from God. Everyone has sinned; me, you, your parents, your neighbor, the President of the United States and yes, even your pastor. The Bible says <u>everyone</u> has sinned.

ROMANS 3:10-12

"There is no one righteous, not even one; there is no one who understands, no one who seeks God. All have turned away......there is no one who does good, not even one."

So, you may be asking yourself, 'How can I get in touch with a holy God if I'm not perfect or have sinned (done wrong things)"? The answer is, you can't stand before a Holy God in your sinful state. You can't fix the problem or make yourself holy on your own good deeds or power. You are broken and need a Savior. Jesus is the only one who does have the power to make you clean enough to approach a Holy God. Sin brings death but Christ brings life.

II CORINTHIANS 5:21

"For God took the sinless Christ and poured into Him our sins. Then, in exchange, he poured God's goodness into us." (LB)

On a mountain of Galilee, Jesus wanted to teach His disciples and the crowd of people listening, all about the Kingdom of God and the true way that a follower of Jesus Christ should live. The word '_BLESSED'_ means happy. When you follow the teachings of Jesus and live out these eight characteristics, you are really happy - not the kind of happiness the world gives, but true happiness that only God can give. In the Beatitudes, Jesus places the primary focus on _attitude._ When you have the right attitude, the correct action will follow. Jesus is focusing on the human heart because your actions reflect what is in your heart. He wants to teach you the way to live in order to please God which results in faithful obedience. You could say that your heart is like toy boxes – full of brokenness; broken attitudes, broken promises, broken standards. But God can fix anything and anyone!

LUKE 6:45

"The good man brings good things out of the good stored up in his heart, and the evil man brings evil things out of the evil stored up in his heart. For out of the overflow of his heart his mouth speaks."

When you acknowledge that you are broken, that you are a sinner and you are empty without Christ, you are also saying that you can be fixed or made new only through God's amazing Grace. He can make you holy. Through His holiness, you have all that God promises; peace, joy, forgiveness and become righteous before God. The kingdom of Heaven is a Kingdom of Grace.

ROMANS 14:17

"The Kingdom of God is not a matter of eating or drinking but of righteousness, peace and joy in the Holy Spirit."

Since the Kingdom of God is for holy people and you're not holy, how do you enter the Kingdom of God? It's as easy as ABC:

- **A**cknowledge you're a sinner
- **B**elieve that Jesus died for your sins and rose again on the third day
- **C**onfess your sins to God and ask for forgiveness

How can you reach God? Actually, humanly you can't but He can reach down to you. God physically brought the Kingdom down to man through Jesus Christ, His Only Begotten Son who, by God's plan, died for the sins of everyone – past, present and future. He invites anyone who is willing to humbly lay aside their own ways and pride and just ask. Just ask Jesus Christ to come in and to dwell in your heart by asking for forgiveness for your sins.

ROMANS 10:9 & 10

"That if you confess with your mouth, 'Jesus is Lord', and believe in your heart that God raised him from the dead, you will be saved. For it is with your heart that you believe and are justified, and it is with your mouth that you confess and are saved."

The Kingdom of God is a perfect and priceless Kingdom and invites all souls to come to Christ. It tells us what God expects from us and what we will expect from Him. God wants to transform your heart; the center of your personality and character. God calls you to faith and discipleship with His Son. Once you make a personal response to Jesus, you will enter the Kingdom of God through the work of Jesus Christ. God will then transform and teach you how to live in the light of God's Kingdom through the Holy Spirit.

In every living soul from Adam to the time we were born, God has placed within us a hunger for Him that can't be filled by anything or anyone else. Whoever chooses to ask Jesus into their hearts will find true satisfaction, meaning and purpose in life. Our happiness comes from being in Christ, who promises to supply every need for the mind, body and soul.

We're all broken and need a Savior. We can't make it on our own. Our good deeds are like filthy rags before a Holy God. We can't see the Kingdom of God on our own merits. It's not based on what we do or not do but on who Jesus Christ is and what He did for us on the Cross.

EPHESIANS 2:8 & 9

"For it is by grace you have been saved, through faith – and this not from ourselves, it is the gift of God – not by works, so that no one can boast."

Society teaches its own version of success and happiness and how to achieve them by promoting pride, power, influence, popularity and pleasing themselves. Society says that these things will bring a painless, quick and easy way to achieve happiness. But the result is empty promises.

These Beatitudes teaches principles for living a successful God-centered, unselfish life that brings happiness and joy that only God can provide. They reveal God's standards that begin in our hearts. They are simply not goals for behavior, but they create a new heart for God and others. When you learn them, an inward transformation takes place, which results in an outward effect; a life that becomes part of the Kingdom of Heaven.

In order to see the Kingdom of God you need to:

_______ Be humble (you can't do it on your own)

_______ Be sorrowful (because of your sinful condition)

_______ Be meek (humble and patient)

_______ Be spiritually hungry (for God and His righteousness)

_______ Be merciful (kind and compassionate)

_______ Be pure in heart (holy before a Holy God)

_______ Be a peacemaker (live at peace with others)

_______ Be willing to stand up for God and others who follow Him

 **"BEE REAL!"**

QUESTION: Which of these eight characteristics on the previous page do you need most, in order to produce these heart attitudes in your life? (Number them 1-8, 1 being the most important)

Write below, a way you can live out the attitude that you chose to be the most important.

____

____

____

BLESSED ARE THE POOR IN SPIRIT

MATTHEW 5:3

***"BLESSED are the poor in spirit,
For theirs is the Kingdom of Heaven."***

As I said in the introduction, we are all broken and need a savior. We can't make it on our own. We can't become holy on our own efforts. We're not perfect. We've done things in our lives that we're sorry for. We've all committed sins against others and against God by doing things that would go against God's Word.

One fact is certain. God is God and we're not. We need God's saving grace and his help to change us from the inside out. We need to admit that we're powerless to make a life change ourselves nor do we have the power to change others, our environment, our past, our harmful habits, our behaviors, or our actions. Only God can efficiently deal with the pain and sorrow that sin has brought into our lives. God never expects us to make it on our own apart from Him, but He wants us to depend on Him for everything and He has a plan for our lives.

The first Beatitude teaches humility. Being poor in spirit means to be humble and that is the starting point to the Christian life and walk in the Spirit. No one comes to God without admitting spiritual poverty. Real poverty isn't your lack of possessions or wealth but it's the sinful heart in need of a Savior.

The world calls poverty as being the lack of physical wealth or required needs. The world says to do your own thing, be self-sufficient and be your own person. But God's Word tells us that spiritual poverty is knowing we can't make it on our own and we turn to God for His help. You can become an heir of God's Kingdom when you realize your spiritual poverty and you have allowed Christ to meet that need.

Since you don't have the power to save yourself, you humbly come to Christ and admit that you have sinned and ask for His forgiveness. God promises that He is faithful and just to forgive you. He desires a living relationship with you, fully trusting in Him every day for all your needs.

I JOHN 1:9

"If we confess our sins, he is faithful and just and will forgive us our sins and purify us from all unrighteousness."

The first step is admitting that you are spiritually poor, give your life to God in true humility by asking for His forgiveness and become totally dependent upon God. You've emptied yourself in order to be filled with Christ and the Holy Spirit in order to live the kind of life God wants you to live.

As I mentioned before, you are not acceptable to God on your own strength, merits or self-righteousness. You cannot be justified by your own abilities, wisdom or energy. You can only be justified through Christ on His righteousness

(Holiness). Only through Him can you come before a Holy God. Through faith you're justified (just as if you had never sinned) and the grace of Christ sanctifies you (continues to keep you Holy) as you live daily in the light of God's Word of truth.

GALATIONS 3:34

"So the law was put in charge to lead us to Christ that we might be justified by faith."

ROMANS 5:1

"Therefore, since we have been justified through faith, we have peace with God through our Lord Jesus Christ."

ROMANS 3:20, 22-24

"No one will be declared righteous in his sight by observing the law; rather, through the law we become conscience of sin. This righteousness from God comes through faith in Jesus Christ to all who believe. There is no difference, for all have sinned and fall short of the glory of God, and we are justified freely by his grace through the redemption that came by Christ Jesus."

So to sum up the first step, we are all sinners. No one can come to the Father, who is righteous and holy, except through faith in Christ who was without sin, because He died for our sins and paid the penalty for sin for us. We are then declared 'not guilty'.

The second step is to realize that you need God's help to live as God would want you to live. You are powerless to control your sin nature, to always follow God's Word and please God in everything you say and do. Once you recognize your poverty state and ask Jesus to come into your heart, He will teach you, through His Word, to exhibit the same attitude as Jesus. As a result, you and those around you will be blessed.

PSALM 146:5

"The Lord God blesses everyone who trusts him and depends on him."

 **"BEE REAL!"**

QUESTION: Have you followed through with the "ABC's"?

(A) Admit you're a sinner
(B) Believe that Jesus died and rose from the dead
(C) Confess your sins & ask God for forgiveness

If you have, write down your experience; include when, where it took place, who helped you come to your decision and how it has affected you:

QUESTION: Read *John 12:12-16, John 13:5* and *Philippians 2:8* and describe how Jesus showed humility in each of these verses.

John 12:12-16

____

____

John 13:5

____

____

Philippians 2:8

____

____

BLESSED ARE THOSE WHO MOURN

MATTHEW 5:4

***"BLESSED are those who mourn,
For they shall be comforted."***

When you mourn and are truly sorrowful because of your sins, God forgives you and comforts you. Genuine repentance will bring comfort to believers. Things you carry around (present or past sins and bad habits) cause grief and pain to yourself and sometimes to others. Some people try to escape from these things by using drugs or alcohol or try to get control through selfishness or anger. When you mourn over your spiritual condition and realize that you need God, you will be comforted and filled with joy.

The world teaches you that doing bad things is ok as long as you don't get caught or blame someone else for your mistakes. Covering sin only results in further sin, sadness and regret. Did you ever do something wrong at home but blame your sister or brother so you wouldn't get in trouble? By not admitting that you did wrong, makes you believe that you can get away with not telling the truth in little things and then later in bigger things. It also causes conflict between you and your siblings. Have you ever cheated on a test at school but never got caught? This one choice may make you believe that you can get away with being dishonest in your future job when you get older. Although you may get away with those kinds of actions, the Heavenly Father sees.

God's Word teaches that there is a special peace and happiness when you admit your mistakes and ask God to forgive them. True repentance is turning from that sin and not wanting to sin again. God will forgive you and remember that sin no more.

The Bible refers to Jesus as a "Man of sorrows" because he was acquainted with grief.

ISAIAH 53:3

"He was despised and rejected by men, a man of sorrows, and familiar with suffering."

Jesus knew what it was to mourn. He was rejected, despised, suffered, carried your sorrows, afflicted, pierced for your transgressions, wounded, oppressed and bore the sins for many. But, He was also sorrowful and mourned over his own people in Jerusalem and all lost souls that were perishing because of sin. His suffering showed His compassion and brought comfort to all who would believe.

PSALM 86:15

"But you, O Lord, are a compassionate and gracious God, slow to anger, abounding in love and faithfulness."

ISAIAH 61:1-2

"The Spirit of the sovereign Lord is upon me, because the Lord has anointed me to preach good news to the

poor. He has sent me to bind up the brokenhearted, to proclaim freedom for the captives and release for the prisoners, to proclaim the year of the Lord's favor and the day of vengeance of our God, to comfort all who mourn."

Because Jesus showed you mercy and comforted you, you need to do the same for others who are also mourning or afflicted. Through your own mourning experience and allowing God to comfort you, you can see others in mourning and need comforting too. You should have compassion for others who are perishing because they don't know the Lord. By drawing close to God's love and His tender and compassionate heart, you allow yourself to be shaped by God and in turn, be drawn to others who are hurt and need the Lord's great mercy.

John 3:16a

"For God so Loved the World that He gave His only Son."

God's love extended to the whole world but what about the world around you? You may not be able to go to every continent but you can see those in mourning around you every day who need a Savior or need to be comforted. Knowing that you can't meet your own needs or the world's needs, you are dependent upon the one who can, and that's God.

This beatitude calls you not only to mourn for your own sin but also for others you may come in contact with. It shows you that as God is compassionate towards you, that you are to be compassionate to others in the world right in front of you; even to the entire world. You can bring comfort to your world by your own actions and attitudes. This may be a daily challenge for you, but ask God to help you open your eyes, open your heart, and be aware of the pain around you so you can respond to others with love, forgiveness, mercy and compassion. By doing this, you can experience the blessedness of God's comfort to yourself and others.

<u>II CORINTHIANS 1:3-5</u>

"Praise be to God and Father of our Lord Jesus Christ, the Father of compassion and the God of all comfort, who comforts us in all our troubles, so that we can comfort those in any trouble with the comfort we ourselves have received from God. For just as the sufferings of Christ flow over into our lives so also through Christ our comfort overflows."

 **_"BEE REAL!"_**

QUESTION: Read **_John: 11:17-44_**. How did Jesus show comfort?

TO MARTHA:

TO MARY:

BLESSED ARE THE MEEK

MATTHEW 5:5

"BLESSED are the meek,
For they shall inherit the earth."

What is being meek? The world may say that meekness is weakness, but God's Word says that when you are meek and humble, you will inherit the Kingdom of God. The word meek means showing humility and patience to others. Other words for meek are kind, gentle, peaceable and submissive. In showing humility towards God and being submissive to Him, you learn to do the same toward others. You submit your will and strength to God's control. When you are submissive to God, it's like a horse with a bridle that the rider controls. The horse is fully yielded to its rider like you would be to God. It's full acceptance of God's plan and direction for you.

Being willing to submit yourself to God is meekness. Seek God's Word, be still and wait on Him and He will reveal how He wants you to show meekness to the world around you.

LUKE 14:11

"For everyone who exalts himself will be humbled,
and he who humbles himself will be exalted."

God speaks of inward beauty, meekness, and wisdom in these verses:

I Peter 3:4

"....It should be that of your inner self, the unfading beauty of a gentle and quiet spirit, which is of great worth of God's sight."

James 3:17

"But the wisdom that comes from Heaven is first of all pure; then peace loving, considerate, submissive, full of mercy and good fruit, impartial and sincere."

What do you do when someone does you wrong? Do you take revenge or do you forgive them? God teaches that when you are meek and humble, you will be willing to overlook their actions against you, forgive them and pray for them. It is God who will judge and is not your place to do so. When you quietly and humbly submit yourself to God and His Word, you will learn to be humble toward others. You'll learn not to take revenge, but forgive when others do you wrong or speak hurtful words toward you. Instead of taking revenge, put your trust and hope in God, who will see justice done. Living this way will not be popular in the world's view but following God's Word and being meek, will bring you blessings and inward happiness.

The Lord Jesus Christ set the example for you. He did not retaliate against those who were beating Him or crucifying Him. He humbled himself even unto death.

<u>*Isaiah 53:7*</u>

"He was oppressed and afflicted, yet he did not open his mouth; he was led like a lamb to the slaughter, and as a sheep before her shearers is silent, so he did not open his mouth."

<u>*Philippians 2:8*</u>

".....He humbled himself and became obedient to death – even death on a cross."

<u>*I Peter 3:9*</u>

"Do not repay evil with evil or insult with insult, but with blessing, because to this you were called so that you may inherit a blessing."

When you face daily choices on how you should respond to situations, you need to decide on whether you want to react the way the world expects you to or how God instructs you. The world would want you to respond with power and authority over others, 'your way or the highway', be first in line, proud, overbearing and stubborn. But God wants you to be humble, gentle, bearing others' burdens, quiet and patient. God's direction will help you to respond as He would want you to respond when situations come your way. Responding with meekness towards others allows the Holy Spirit's gentleness to flow out to others, which will also lead them to inherit God's Kingdom.

 **"BEE REAL!"**

QUESTION: How did Christ show meekness in these verses?

Matthew 11:28-30

I Peter 2: 22, 23

QUESTION: Who could you show meekness to and how could you do that?

BLESSED WHO HUNGER AND THIRST FOR RIGHTEOUSNESS

MATTHEW 5:1-11

"BLESSED are those who hunger and thirst for righteousness,
For they will be filled."

Everyone hungers for physical food and water because our bodies require the proper nourishment to survive. However, when God says to hunger and thirst after righteousness, He means to desire spiritual nourishment through His Word and His righteousness, which only He can provide. You need to desire God and his righteousness just as you desire your favorite food or drink. It means to grow in Christ so you can be filled with His Spirit, in order to live according to how He would want you to live. When Jesus was tempted in the desert by Satan, Satan tempted Him to turn the stones to bread because by then, Jesus would have been very hungry. But Jesus replied:

Matthew 4:4

"It is written; man does not live by bread alone but by every word that comes from the mouth of God."

It is important to feed on God's Word by attending church and hanging around your Christian friends. But more important than these, is having a quiet time reading God's Word every day – not just on Sunday. Only God's Word can fill your life with joy and fill your empty soul with hope.

<u>**Psalm 107:9**</u>

"For He satisfies the thirsty and fills the hungry with good things."

When you first asked Jesus into your heart to become Savior and Lord of your life, you fed on spiritual "milk" of the Word, just as newborn babies would feed on physical milk and then later physical meat. This would help them grow strong and mature physically. As you grow in Christ, you'll need to move from "milk" to "meat" of His Word to help you grow spiritually. God's Word helps you to grow your faith strong and brings spiritual maturity. Without this maturity, your faith is weak and you will not be able to do all these things He wants you to do. Continual prayer and study of God's Word results in a deeper walk with the Lord.

<u>*I Peter 2:2*</u>

"Like newborn babies, crave pure spiritual milk, so that by it you may grow up in your salvation, now that you have tasted that the Lord is good."

<u>*Hebrews 5:13 & 14*</u>

"Anyone who lives on milk, being still an infant, is not acquainted with the teaching about righteousness. But solid food is for the mature, who by constant use have trained themselves to distinguish good from evil."

Feeding on the meat of God's Word will train you to know good from evil and bring spiritual maturity, so you can live out God's Word in your lives. Living out God's Word means that with maturity you'll do what Jesus taught:

- <u>Love God and love others</u> – **(Matthew 22:37, 39) "Love the Lord your God with all your heart and with all your soul and with all your mind and love your neighbor as yourself."**
- <u>Faith alone</u> – *(Hebrews 11: 1) "Now Faith is being sure of what we hope for and certain of what we do not see."*
- <u>Put God first place above all else</u> - *(Matthew 6:33a) "But seek first the kingdom and his righteousness."*
- <u>Forgive</u> – *(Colossians 3:13) "Be gentle and ready to forgive; never hold grudges. Remember, the Lord forgave you, so you must forgive others." (LB)*
- <u>Pray always</u> – *(I Thessalonians 5:17) "Pray continuously."*
- <u>Seek wisdom</u> – *(Matthew 7:23) "Therefore everyone who hears these words of mine and puts them into practice is like a wise man who built his house on the rock."*

The world says to hunger and thirst after money and power because they will bring happiness and fulfillment. It says to get yours while you can. Many try to fill their empty lives with worldly things; money, power, popularity and greed. But when you hunger and thirst after His righteousness instead of the worldly things, peace, fulfillment and happiness will follow. By seeking Him with your whole heart and putting Him first in your life, He will provide everything you need. When you do this, you will not be seeking worldly things but you'll seek them from God, who will provide you with all things

Hungering and thirsting for Righteousness means that you know you need a relationship with God and that His Word of Truth can only fill the void in your life. You will be right with God and with other people. You will be reflecting God in your attitude, character and through your actions. However, it may be a little scary for you because that means that when you fully focus on God and His Word, God will change your thoughts and affections. Fully opening yourself to God will change your life. You must continually hunger and thirst for God daily, not just when you first believed. Every day will bring a different situation where you will need God's presence and grace. Your awareness of needing God's grace will also make you aware of others who need it too.

God is faithful. When you seek Him and His righteousness, He will fill you to overflowing so it can flow to others. You were created to fill your life with God and have a relationship with him. Open your heart and allow Him to lead you to share this truth with someone else.

The book of Proverbs is full of God's wisdom. Throughout the book, God tells you everything you'll need for living a righteous and wise life. Here are some examples:

- ❖ OBEY PARENTS (1:8-9)
- ❖ AVOID BAD COMPANY (1:10-19)
- ❖ BE KIND TO OTHERS (3:27-35)
- ❖ GUARD YOUR HEART (4:23-27)
- ❖ DO NOT BE LAZY (10:4)
- ❖ CHEATING AND DISHONESTY (11:1)
- ❖ PRIDE AND HUMILITY (11:2)
- ❖ GENTLE ANSWERS (15:1)
- ❖ BEING KIND TO THE POOR (19:17)
- ❖ LYING (24:28)

 **"BEE REAL!"**

QUESTION: Read **Hebrews 5:13 & 14**. What is the result of living on milk and living on solid food?

MILK: Not acquainted with

____

SOLID FOOD: To distinguish

____

QUESTION: In **Romans 14:17** the Kingdom of Heaven is what three things:

1.

2.

3.

BLESSED ARE THE MERCIFUL

MATTHEW 5:7

"BLESSED are the merciful,
For they will be shown mercy."

The first three Beatitudes; poor in spirit, mourning, hungering and thirsting showed inward action. The last one showed submission to God and learning to show meekness towards others. This one involves positive action by showing mercy to others because God was merciful to you.

To show mercy is to show compassion and kindness to others; even though they don't really deserve it. Being merciful also means forgiveness for others who do you wrong even when they don't deserve it. In that way, you are really showing God's grace, forgiveness and love to them. Humanly when others do you wrong, you want to get mad and sometimes get even. But as this scripture shows, God will be merciful to you when you are merciful to others. Everyone needs mercy. Do not get angry, take revenge and get back at them. God's Word teaches you how you are to treat others because of God's mercy towards you.

I CORINTHIANS 13:4-8a

"Love is patient, love is kind. It does not envy, it does not boast, it is not proud. It is not rude, it is not self-seeking, it is not easily angered, it keeps no record of wrongs. Love does not delight in evil but rejoices

with the truth. It always protects, always trusts, always hopes, always perseveres. Love never fails."

GALATIONS 5:22

"But the fruits of the Spirit is love, joy, peace, patience, kindness, goodness, faithfulness, gentleness and self-control."

MICAH 6:8

"He has showed you, O man, what is good. And what does the Lord require of you? To act justly and to love mercy and to walk humbly with your God."

Being merciful can also mean to show sympathy toward others' hardships, to care and comfort others, being willing to help others who are in need and show goodness and love when other people aren't nice to you. Mercy is a choice and it takes practice. When you go through your daily routine, there will be situations where you can react with criticism and judgment, or you can choose to show God's grace and mercy. Continually connecting to God, you will remain open to see those around you who need God's mercy too. It's a choice to do something good with what God blessed you with.

God shows great love and mercy towards you; even when you don't deserve it. He reveals His mercy when you mess up and make mistakes. He shows you mercy when you experience difficulties or loss in your life. Therefore you should show this same mercy to others even if they don't deserve it.

Jesus is our high priest who can sympathize with our weaknesses. When you come before His throne you will find mercy and grace to help you in your time of need.

Hebrews 4:14-16

"Therefore, since we have a great high priest who has gone through the heavens, Jesus the Son of God, let us hold firmly to the faith we profess. For we do not have a high priest who is unable to sympathize with our weaknesses, but we have one who has been tempted in every way, just as we are – yet was without sin. Let us then approach the throne of grace with confidence, so that we may receive mercy and find grace to help us in our time of need."

James 5:11

"The Lord is full of compassion and mercy."
Acts 2:21

"Anyone who asks for mercy from the Lord shall have it and shall be saved."

In Colossians, God instructs you not only to show kindness and compassion but to forgive others as Christ has forgiven you. As the Lord has shown you compassion, mercy and forgiveness, he wants you to do the same toward others.

<u>*Colossians 3:12-14*</u>

"Therefore, as God's chosen people, holy and dearly loved, clothe yourselves with compassion, kindness, humility, gentleness and patience. Bear with each other and forgive whatever grievances you may have against one another. Forgive as the Lord forgave you."

It's easy to be kind to those who are kind to you but you'll have to admit it's very hard to be kind to those who aren't kind to you. Jesus taught that you should turn the other cheek by turning away when others do you wrong, instead of getting them back by being mean to them. The world says to take revenge on those who have hurt you but Jesus taught forgiveness and kindness toward others, despite their evil deeds.

Ephesians 4:32

"Be kind and compassionate to one another, forgiving each other, just as in Christ, God forgave you."

 **"BEE REAL!"**

QUESTION: Read **Titus 3:3-8**. List the changes that occurred in your heart and life as a result of salvation through Christ Jesus; not through your own efforts, but because of His mercy. You can only show mercy with God's help.

RENEWAL _______________________________________

JUSTIFIED_______________________________________

BECOME ____

HOPE ____

DEVOTE____

QUESTION: In **Matthew 5:43-47** Jesus talks about loving your enemies and why it makes a difference. List them below.

WORLD VIEW   GOD'S VIEW

BLESSED ARE THE PURE IN HEART

MATTHEW 5:8

**"BLESSED are the pure in heart,
For they shall see God."**

When you think of the word pure, you probably think of all the things that this world claims to be pure:

> ➢ Pure chocolate
> ➢ Pure hand sanitizers
> ➢ Pure water

Being pure means to be free from contamination or without faults; perfect. Unfortunately as much as this world tries to make things pure, the reality is that nothing is perfect here in this world and neither are you. But through salvation, you are perfect through Jesus Christ but that doesn't mean that you won't make mistakes. The Holy Spirit can transform you daily to walk perfect in His sight.

Ecclesiastes 7:20

"There is not a righteous man on earth who does what is right and never sins."

You can see by this verse that no one is righteous (perfect) here on this earth. But Christ is, and through Him, you can be too.

<u>**Hebrews 7:26**</u>

"Such a high priest [Jesus] meets our need-one who is holy, blameless, pure, set apart from sinners, exalted above the heavens."

<u>**I Corinthians 6:11b**</u>

"But you were washed, you were sanctified, you were justified in the name of the Lord Jesus Christ and by the Spirit of our God."

Spiritual purity means being transformed from the inside out. It means being <u>justified</u>; "just as if you never sinned". It declares you righteous because of what Jesus did for you and puts you in perfect standing with a Holy God. Jesus was able to do this because he was perfect and without blemish **(I Peter 1:19)**.

Being <u>sanctified</u> has to do with your character and conduct. It's what God does within you to promote a good relationship with Him and others.

When God saves you from your sins, the Holy Spirit dwells within you to purify you inwardly so you can act that way outwardly. The Spirit, through His Word, will purify your heart from fleshly thoughts and desires and conform you to a new life in Christ, which will set your heart toward honoring God in all you do and say.

<u>***Romans 12:2***</u>

"Do not conform any longer to the pattern of this world, but be transformed by the renewing of your mind. Then you will be able to and approve what God's will is – His good, pleasing and perfect will."

<u>**Philippians 4:8**</u>

"Whatever is true, whatever is noble, whatever is right, whatever is pure, whatever is lovely, whatever is admirable – if anything is excellent or praiseworthy – think about such things."

God not only wants to save your soul from spiritual death but He also wants to create in you a clean and pure heart and mind. God doesn't want you to continue down the same path as the unsaved but He wants to develop in you the same characteristics of Jesus – true, noble, right and pure. How do you do that? You certainly can't do that on your own. You need the help of your Savior and Holy Spirit when you surrender your life to Jesus, study His Word and heed to the Holy Spirit's teaching. You need God's help and guidance to do everything with the right motive; pure in heart. You need to allow God to work within you and change you from the inside out at the center of seeking a pure heart.

To give you a visual example, think of a potter forming and molding a clay pot. The clay cannot tell the potter what shape he will be. The potter makes that choice as to the shape of the pot. Just like that pot, the Bible says that He is the potter and we are the clay. God wants to mold you and create in you a heart that is pure to seek God, to fill your heart with one purpose and to deepen your desire for Him.

Isaiah 64:8

"O Lord, you are our Father. We are the clay, you are the potter; we are all the work of your hands."

When you remain in the Lord, dedicate yourself to a relationship with Him, and use your gifts and skills for His purpose and plan, He will meet you where you are. He will richly bless you with continual pureness of heart and He promises that you will see the Kingdom of God.

 **"BEE REAL!"**

QUESTION: **In II Corinthians 7:1,** Paul tells us to **"*purify ourselves from everything that contaminates the body and spirit, perfecting holiness out of reverence for God.*"** List below those things that could contaminate the body and spirit; then list ways to show reverence to God.

Contaminate body and spirit

Reverence for God

QUESTION: Read **I Timothy 1:5** and give every day examples of having a pure heart, good conscience and a sincere faith.

<u>PURE HEART</u>:

<u>GOOD CONSCIENCE</u>:

<u>SINCERE FAITH</u>:

<u>BLESSED ARE THE PEACEMAKERS</u>

<u>*MATTHEW 5:9*</u>

*"BLESSED are the peacemakers,
For they shall be called sons of God."*

Peace is defined as calm, harmony and restful. As you look around you, you certainly don't see a lot of peace. Peace is definitely lacking in homes, communities, in our nation and in the world. Fighting and conflict surrounds you everywhere.

True peace comes from the Father. First and foremost, you must have peace with God through Jesus Christ, who is the Prince of Peace.

<u>*Isaiah 9:6*</u>

"For to us a child is born, to us a son is given, and the government will be on His shoulders. And He will be called Wonderful Counselor, Mighty God, Everlasting Father, Prince of Peace."

Jesus came to bring peace on earth and to all who believe in Him. God promises that when you accept Christ as your personal Savior, He will give personal peace, despite what is going on around you. This kind of peace brings salvation and healing. God wants to free you and the world from everything that brings chaos. In the book of John,

Jesus comforted His disciples before He left them to go back to Heaven. God also comforts you in these verses.

Psalm 29:11

"The Lord gives strength to his people; the Lord blesses his people with peace."

John 16:33

"I have told you these things, so that in me you may have peace. In this world you will have trouble. But take heart! I have overcome the world."

By acknowledging your own poverty and need for peace, you can see others' need for peace as well. Once you've received God's peace in your own life, God wants you to show that peace to others. As much as possible, be peaceful towards others. God encourages you to do just that in these verses below.

Romans 12:18

"If it is possible, as far as it depends on you, live at peace with everyone."

I Corinthians 7:15

"God has called us to live in peace."

<u>*I Corinthians 14:33*</u>

"For God is not a God of disorder but of peace"

How can you demonstrate peace towards others? You can be cool when others are hot and give a gentle answer instead of arguing with others. Sometimes it means reconciliation (make peace).

<u>**Proverbs 15:1**</u>

"A soft answer turns away (avoids) wrath (strife), but harsh words cause quarrels."

Living at peace with others is one way to show that Jesus Christ rules in your heart and is one of the Fruits of the Spirit. It is an outward sign of an inward change. The attitude of peace in your own life will radiate to the chaotic world around you. Peacemaking is an active way to invest your time and energy. By seeking peace with God in your own life and showing it toward others, you are identified as God's sons and daughters.

<u>**Galatians 5:22**</u>

"But the Fruit of the Spirit is love, joy, <u>peace</u>, patience, kindness, goodness, faithfulness, gentleness and self-control."

 **"BEE REAL!"**

QUESTION: Read **Romans 8:5 and 6**. List the results of having your mind set on the sinful nature and having your mind set on the Holy Spirit:

<u>Sinful Nature:</u>

<u>Holy Spirit:</u>

QUESTION: Read **James 3:17 and 18** and list what God can give you through God's wisdom.

P ____________________

P ____________ L ____________

C __________________

S __________________

F ___________ of M ________________

G _________ F __________

I __________________

S _______________

James 3:18

"Peacemakers who sow in peace raise a harvest of righteousness."

BLESSED ARE THE PERSECUTED

MATTHEW 5:10

***"BLESSED** are those who are persecuted because of righteousness,*
    For theirs is the kingdom of heaven."

***"BLESSED** are you when people insult you, persecute you and falsely say all kinds of evil against you because of me. Rejoice and be glad, because great is your reward in heaven, for in the same way they persecuted the prophets who were before you."*

You usually don't hear about persecution because of faith in God and being a Christian in this country. It's heard mostly in other countries. However, unfortunately it exists everywhere. Even here in the United States many believers experience discrimination in jobs, housing and the legal system; sometimes at your school or in your neighborhood. To stand up for your faith in Jesus takes real guts in the face of persecution. It's real easy to take the high road, go with the crowd or conform to your friends' beliefs and avoid the pain and embarrassment of being harassed.

In this Beatitude, Jesus was teaching his followers how to deal with difficult circumstances. Jesus knew that if some of the people hated Him, that they would also hate those who believe in Him. They also persecuted the prophets long ago long before Jesus walked on the earth. But Jesus is reassuring them and you to rejoice when others persecute you because of your faith in Jesus. Rewards will follow for those who are persecuted for the sake of Christ.

After Jesus died and rose again to Heaven, all of his apostles and many other believers continued telling others about Jesus, despite being persecuted. Some were put in prison and some were killed for their testimony. The religious leaders were especially persistent to stop them from talking about Jesus in public. But despite the persecution, the believers rejoiced and kept witnessing about Jesus. There was one in particular who had an extreme hate towards them. He was a Pharisee and his name was Saul of Tarsus.

Saul was extremely against those who believed in Jesus and went to the high priest and asked for permission to go to the synagogue (church) in Damascus to arrest the believers and take them as prisoners to Jerusalem. Once that permission was granted, he immediately left with some soldiers and headed for Damascus. But God had other plans.

ACTS 9:3–5

"As he neared Damascus on his journey, suddenly a light from heaven flashed around him. He fell to the ground and heard a voice say to him, 'Saul, Saul, why do you persecute me?' 'Who are you, Lord?' Saul asked. 'I am Jesus, whom you are persecuting.' He

**replied. *Now get up and go into the city and you will
be told what you must do.'***

Saul had a personal encounter with the Lord Jesus.
He went to the city and was told through a disciple named
Ananias that God chose him to go to the Gentiles (believers
who weren't Jews) and tell them about Jesus and that he
would suffer for Jesus' name. These were the same believers
that he was going to persecute and arrest! Saul's heart and
life was changed and so was his name. Saul's name was
changed to Paul and immediately, he started preaching in
the synagogue about Jesus. Up to that point, his whole life
was about persecuting those who believed in Jesus, but he
would soon find out that he too would be persecuted greatly
for the name of Jesus.

The following are just some of the persecution that Paul
endured **(II Corinthians 11:24-27)**.

- ✓ Five times received from the Jews forty lashes minus
  one
- ✓ Three times beaten with rods
- ✓ Once stoned and left for dead
- ✓ Three times shipwrecked
- ✓ Knew hunger and thirst

More than likely, you won't have to experience these
same hardships but you may have to be ridiculed by your
friends for believing in Jesus. But if you do, God's word says
that you will be rewarded in the Kingdom of Heaven. Paul
knew the consequences of his faith, but he did it anyway for
the sake of knowing Christ and telling others about Him. He

knew that his reward is not here on earth but in Heaven. He knew that nothing can separate him from the love of God and that he could do all things through Christ. Paul lived and died knowing the Savior and depending upon His Word and His promises.

Regarding suffering, Paul says............

PHILIPPIANS 1:21

"To live is Christ, to die is gain."

ROMANS 8:18

"I consider that our present sufferings are not worth comparing to the glory that will be revealed in us."

Romans 8:35-38

"Who shall separate us from the love of Christ? Shall trouble or hardship or persecution or famine or danger or sword? As it is written, 'For your sake we face death all day long; we are considered as sheep to be slaughtered.' No, in all these things we are more than conquerors through Him who loved us. For I am convinced that neither death nor life, neither angels nor demons, neither the present nor the future, nor any powers, neither height nor depth, nor anything else in all creation, will be able to separate us from the love of God that is in Christ Jesus our Lord."

 **"BEE REAL!"**

QUESTION: Read about these two men of faith in the midst of persecution.

<u>Daniel</u>: The king issued a decree that no one was allowed to pray to any other god except to him, but Daniel believed in God alone and got down on his knees and prayed three times a day giving thanks to God.

Read Daniel 6:13; 16-23. What did Daniel do in the face of persecution and what was the outcome?

Stephen: In the book of Acts, Stephen loved God more than anything else and he went around telling others about Jesus. But like many other believers, he was persecuted for his belief.

Read Acts 6:8-15 and describe Stephen's Godly qualities and how people reacted to his faith in God.

Read Acts 7:54-60 and describe Stephen's reaction when he was persecuted.

QUESTION: What do you do when you are persecuted or ridiculed for your belief in Jesus? What do you do when you see someone else being persecuted or ridiculed for their belief in Jesus? How can you stand up for them?

<u>***CONCLUSION***</u>

So, what did you learn from these Beatitudes and how can you put what you've learned into action?

First of all, you learned that you aren't perfect and that you need to ask God to forgive you of your sins in order to approach a Holy God. Secondly, you learned in this guide about how you are blessed by God when you follow His Word and how you can bless others.

The first Beatitude taught you humility. The starting point is being poor in spirit, which means being humble before God. No one comes to God without admitting spiritual poverty. You can't change on your own power; you need God's help.

The second Beatitude taught you to mourn and be truly sorrowful because of your sins. When you come to God with that humble attitude, God will forgive you. Genuine repentance will bring you comfort knowing that God has forgiven your past, present and even your future sins.

The third Beatitude taught you that meekness isn't weakness but rather being willing to submit yourself to God. By seeking God through His Word and prayer, He will reveal how He wants you to show meekness to the world around you.

The fourth Beatitude taught you that when you hunger and thirst after God and His Righteousness, you will have a right relationship with God and with others. You will learn to reflect God in your character through your actions to others.

The fifth Beatitude taught you that with God's help, you can show mercy, compassion and kindness to others; even though they don't really deserve it. You can also learn to forgive those who have done you wrong rather than taking revenge. In that way, you are really showing God's grace, forgiveness and love to them.

The sixth Beatitude taught you that you can become spiritually pure, which means being transformed from the inside out through God's Word. Being pure means that you are justified and you are declared righteous because of what Jesus did for you on the cross and puts you in perfect standing with a Holy God.

The seventh Beatitude taught you that by acknowledging your own need for peace, you can see others' need for peace as well. By seeking God and His peace, you too can be a peacemaker in the world around you. True peace only comes from the Father through Jesus Christ, who is the Prince of Peace.

The eighth Beatitude taught you that standing up for what you believe and sharing your faith with others may bring persecution. But like many who faced persecutions for their faith, God has promised great rewards in Heaven.

These Beatitudes taught you that God will bless you when your attitudes line up with God's Word. When you allow Jesus to change you from the inside out and grow into the kind of person He wants you to be, you find yourself happier and more at peace. And when that happens, you will reflect Jesus to everyone around you and as result, the Kingdom of Heaven will be seen here on earth.

 ***"BEE REAL!"***

QUESTION: What are the true characteristics of a follower of Jesus in the following verses?

JOHN 3:5

"Unless one is born of _____________ and of the

_____________, he cannot enter the Kingdom of God."

II PETER 3:18

"Grow in the _______________ and ________________

of our Lord and Savior Jesus Christ."

COLOSSIANS 2:6

"So then, just as you received Christ Jesus as Lord,

continue to ________ in Him, _____________ and

__________________ in Him, ________________

in the _____________ as you were taught."

II PETER 1:5 – 6

"For this reason, make every effort to add to your

faith ________________; and to goodness

________________; and to knowledge;

________________; and to self-control,

________________; and to perseverance,

________________."

COLOSSIANS 2:6

'So then, just as you received Christ Jesus as Lord,

________________ to live in Him, ________________,

and ________________ ________ in Him,

________________ in the faith as you were

taught, and overflowing with ________________."